Potbellied Pigs

by Julie Murray

Abdo Kids Jumbo is an Imprint of Abdo Kids
abdobooks.com

abdobooks.com

Published by Abdo Kids, a division of ABDO, P.O. Box 398166, Minneapolis, Minnesota 55439.

Printed in the United States of America, North Mankato, Minnesota.

052025

092025

Photo Credits: Adobe Stock, Alamy, Getty Images, Minden Pictures, Science Source, Shutterstock

Production Contributors: Teddy Borth, Jennie Forsberg, Grace Hansen
Design Contributors: Candice Keimig, Pakou Moua

Library of Congress Control Number: 2024947622

Publisher's Cataloging-in-Publication Data

Names: Murray, Julie, author.

Title: Potbellied pigs / by Julie Murray

Description: Minneapolis, Minnesota : Abdo Kids, 2026 | Series: Fancy farm animals | Includes online resources and index.

Identifiers: ISBN 9798384905257 (lib. bdg.) | ISBN 9798384905950 (ebook) | ISBN 9798384906308 (Read-to-me ebook)

Subjects: LCSH: Potbellied pig--Juvenile literature. | Swine--Juvenile literature. | Farm animals--Juvenile literature. | Livestock--Juvenile literature. | Domestic animals--Juvenile literature.

Classification: DDC 636.4--dc23

Table of Contents

Potbellied Pigs

Potbellied pigs are a smaller version of standard pigs. They are friendly, smart, and cute. It's no wonder they are popular fancy farm animals!

Potbellied pigs were **bred** from wild pigs in Vietnam. Farmers bred them for their meat. Potbellied pigs were easier to care for because of their smaller size. They were brought to the United States in the 1980s.

Asia
Vietnam
N
S
E
W

Today, most potbellied pigs live on farms. Some are even kept as house pets. They are very smart animals. They can learn to do tricks and be potty trained!

Body

Even though potbellied pigs are small pigs, they still grow big! They stand 1.5 feet (0.5 m) tall and are 3 feet (0.9 m) long. They can weigh from 100 to 200 pounds (45 to 91 kg).

Potbellied pigs have a round body and short legs. Their skin is covered in **coarse** hair. They have a short **snout**, upright ears, and a straight tail.

Potbellied pigs were first **bred** to be all black in color. Today, they can be solid black, white, silver, or pink. They can also be spotted.

Diet

Potbellied pigs have a strong sense of smell. They search for food in the dirt. They use their **snout** to dig up the food.

On the farm, potbellied pigs eat special pig food. They also eat vegetables, fruit, and hay. They dig through the dirt to find worms and insects too.

Baby Potbellied Pigs

Female potbellied pigs have 1 to 12 babies at a time. Baby pigs are called piglets. Piglets weigh about 7 pounds (3.2 kg) at birth. Potbellied pigs can live for 20 years.

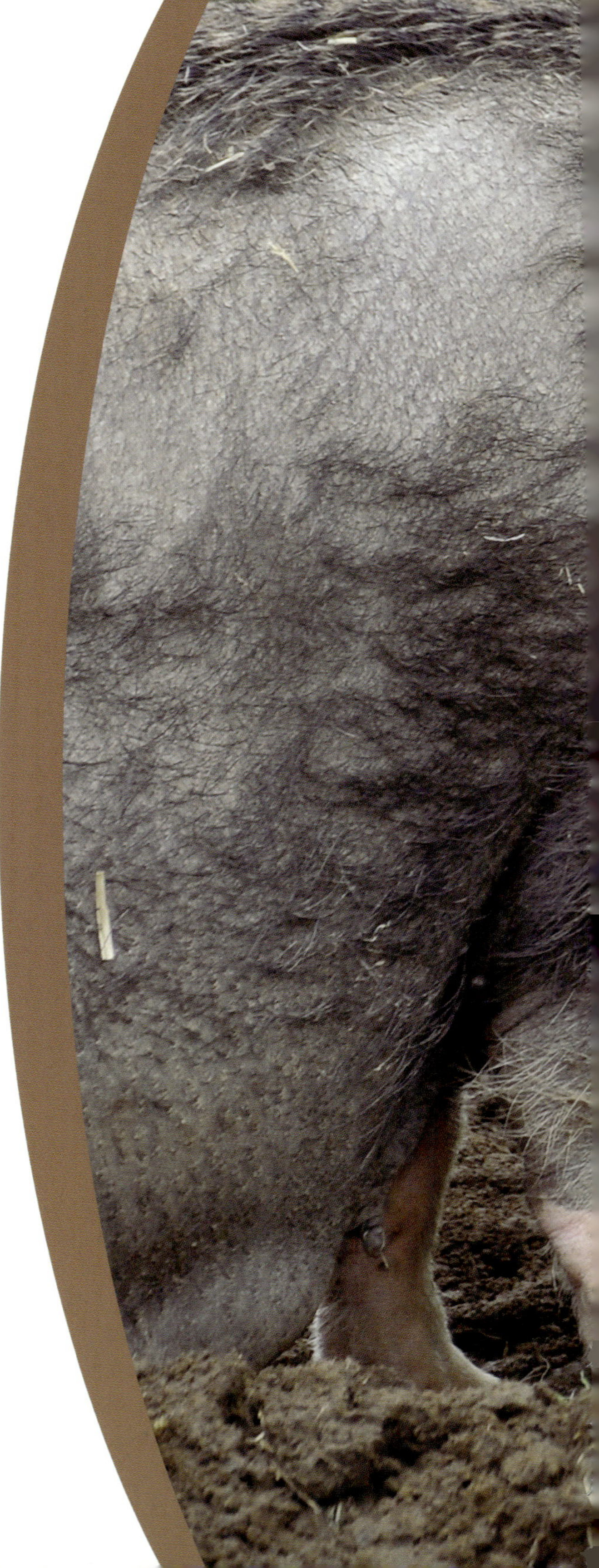

More Facts

- Potbellied pigs are also known as Vietnamese or Asian potbellied pigs.

- They are **social** animals. They need the company of other pigs or humans.

- Potbellied pigs make lots of noises to communicate. They squeal, whine, **grunt**, and scream. They can be very loud!

Glossary

bred – developed an animal over time for a certain purpose.

coarse – rough to the touch.

grunt – a short, deep sound like that made by a hog.

snout – the part of an animal's head that sticks out. The snout includes the nose, mouth, and jaws.

social – living in groups instead of alone.

Index